The Mentor

A Business Parable

Gil Weinreich

Weinreich Communications Press

Copyright © 2020 by Weinreich Communications, Ltd. All rights reserved.

Published by Weinreich Communications Press
weinreichcommunications@gmail.com

ISBN: 9798653939440 (softcover)

Cover Designer: Dragan Bilic

TABLE OF CONTENTS

PREFACE	4
ACT I	6
SCENE 1	6
SCENE 2	10
SCENE 3	13
ACT II	19
SCENE 1	19
SCENE 2	23
SCENE 3	26
ACT III	36
SCENE 1	36
SCENE 2	45
SCENE 3	49
ACT IV	54
SCENE 1	54
SCENE 2	61
SCENE 3	69
AFTERWORD	75
ABOUT THE AUTHOR	78

PREFACE

I wrote this parable to help financial advisors, and those who aspire to become one, become happier and more successful. Advisors are all too often made to feel a tension between helping the client and helping themselves, when those two objectives could be in complete harmony. The corporations for which they work subtly, or not so subtly, pressure them to sell. This sales pressure can be highly alienating, especially to new advisors who were attracted to their jobs because they wanted to use their knowledge of financial markets and innate talents in financial planning to help people. The goal of helping people gets lost when the advisor's focus is diverted to the achievement of productivity and efficiency to an extent that subtracts value for the client and enjoyment from the life of the advisor.

But it needn't be this way. After more than two decades of first-hand observation of this industry – 18 years at Research / ThinkAdvisor, and four years at Seeking Alpha – I thought the time has come to lay out these issues. But, why do so in a play, of all formats? My reasoning is that financial advisors, possibly the most marketed-to profession, are daily flooded with an ocean of words from the media and their own industry. Even the best of this content is ever falling into the memory hole as new waves of information resume their daily barrage. Therein lies the value of fiction, and especially a parable stripped down to the core. By embodying key ideas in a story, those ideas, literally and literarily, take on a life of their own and lodge themselves in the reader's heart.

My intention is that through a short investment of time and imagination, financial advisors can decide whether they prefer to receive their business advice from a Jacob

Pelowitz or a Robert Stephenson, and whether their career trajectory should rocket like Reggie's or be balanced like Benjamin's. In short, a fictional story offers the advantage of making key ideas vivid and crystallizes the choices faced by readers.

Events reach a crescendo by the play's end – in the sort of drama that every financial advisor will face in his or her career. Real-life drama of this kinds presents us all with a moment of truth: Have I achieved my goals? Have I achieved them at somebody else's expense? Is this really the kind of career I want to have or the life I want to lead? I especially hope that young or aspiring financial advisors will read this play, to think about these issues *before* they arise and to choose a life of happiness and honor and not one that may lead to regret.

I gratefully acknowledge the acquaintances I have made in my career as a financial journalist – the noble ones and shallow ones, the arrogant and the absurd – who enabled me to populate this play with characters both realistic and humorous. And I thank my wife Nedra, son Ariel and daughter Moriah for their sharp comments and criticisms, which greatly enhanced the play's ultimate form.

Gil Weinreich
Jerusalem, Israel

ACT I

SCENE 1

Orientation for advisor training at Tilden Prescott Global Wealth Management

MARK MACHER, senior managing director for advisor training, addresses a group of new advisor recruits before formal training begins, his Brooks Brothers suit at odds with his demeanor of a PE coach lacking empathy for the least athletic of his charges.

MACHER

As we wrap up this orientation, I want to introduce you to what I like to call "the three threes."

In *three* years from now, just *three* out of 10 of you will still be in this business: the ones who successfully pass through *three* gates.

You reach the first gate after three months of training, when some of you conclude: "This isn't for me."

You reach the second gate after one year, when another bunch of you will understand the meaning of "you don't sell, you don't eat."

And you reach the third gate after three years, when another wave of you will drop out. I'll tell you right now who those will be: The ones who have nobody left to talk to. If you don't have a big pipeline of prospects in three years, you'll have no future at Tilden Prescott, or anywhere else in this business.

THE MENTOR | 7

MACHER gulps some water and glances at a roster of the new advisor trainees in his charge.

I expect to see all 30 of you tomorrow morning at eight o'clock, for our first day of training – on time.

pauses meaningfully

And I expect to see nine of you still here three years from now.

Two trainees, Benjamin Pearl and his friend Reggie Gleam, leave the orientation together.

BENJAMIN

sarcastically

Well, that was encouraging.

REGGIE

There's nothing to worry about, Benjamin. Three-fifths of one of us will be on his way to great financial success three years from now.

BENJAMIN

No doubt you'll make it into the winners' circle, Reggie. Your wall full of awards and Kung Fu black belt all say so.

REGGIE

You were no slouch in the classes we took together at UCLA. So why worry? What's the difference?

BENJAMIN

There's a big difference. If I got a B in history, I still enjoyed the class and learned something. If I get a B in advisor training, I'll apparently starve.

REGGIE

Then don't get a B. Buck yourself up and be one of the ones who make it.

BENJAMIN

I'm willing to work hard, but I didn't like Macher's presentation. It felt cold and competitive.

REGGIE

I've got news for you, Benjamin. Life is often cold and competitive – especially in areas like wealth management, where there's a lot of money to be made. What Macher was saying is if you work hard, you'll have a future in this business.

BENJAMIN

To the contrary. If you work hard, it's possible you *won't* have a future in this business, but you *may* succeed at obliterating three years of your life finding out the difference between winning the bronze medal and achieving nothing.

REGGIE

Then go for the gold, my friend. If you end up with silver, you'll still be happy.

BENJAMIN

I'm not giving up, Reggie. I'll see you tomorrow.

The two part ways. Benjamin fumbles for his phone and dials a number.

RECEPTIONIST

heard over the phone

Tilden Prescott Advisors, how may I help you?

BENJAMIN

Hello. I'm trying to reach an advisor by the name of Joseph Pelowitz.

PELOWITZ

answering call transfer

Joseph Pelowitz...

BENJAMIN

Mr. Pelowitz, this is Jack Pearl's son, Benjamin. My father suggested I call you to get your advice. He speaks very highly of you and since I was aiming to join your profession, he thought you'd be a good person to offer a few pointers. Truth be told, I like doing things on my own and wasn't planning on taking up my dad's suggestion. But the orientation I had today at Tilden Prescott made me rethink the wisdom of relying on my own wits. Would you be free to speak with me about this some time?

PELOWITZ

Hey, great to hear from you, Benjamin. Your father's a good friend, and it would be my pleasure to help any way I can. I've got an open slot this afternoon at 4 p.m. If you're free then, stop by my office at Wilshire and Beverly Drive. I'm on the seventh floor.

BENJAMIN

Thank you, Mr. Pelowitz. I really appreciate your willingness to help. I'll see you later today then.

SCENE 2

BENJAMIN briefs PELOWITZ on his orientation.

BENJAMIN

So I found the experience disconcerting and more than a bit off-putting. I have a good grasp of markets – above average. I feel I could help people plan for their financial futures. But Macher made it sound like it's all about smiling and dialing, about achieving quotas, about pumping people for referrals. I want to help people, and he took all the joy out of that vision.

PELOWITZ

You're right to feel concerned, Benjamin. And you're right that Macher and pretty much everybody else in the industry want to turn you into a productivity robot. They're right, of course, that building a business takes effort. You should listen carefully to their recommendations. But here's the good news: You can apply their guidance selectively while remaining faithful to your own vision.

BENJAMIN

I like this approach!

PELOWITZ

It's really the *only* approach. They're going to suggest a hundred different things to do. Nobody can do all of them. I know a young gal in the same training group as you –

Sophie Mandel – who happens to hate sales. You wouldn't think she's a candidate for this business. But she's determined to make it her career. True, you can't build a financial advisory practice – or any business – without business development and sales, but you can do it your way. And that's the only way that will ever work over the long run.

BENJAMIN

That's encouraging. But specifically, how do you think someone like me, or Sophie for that matter, could do this? I enjoy seeing personal finance as a puzzle. I like to figure out how to optimize outcomes based on the whole gamut of identifying goals, sensible asset allocation, intelligent spending, tax efficiency and so forth. Who's going to knock on my door for that? And why would they pay an advisory fee, which they may see as *subtracting* from their wealth, if their goal is to *increase* their wealth?

PELOWITZ

Are you kidding? That's what people need – and want! That's what my clients pay me for. Maybe they won't exactly knock on your door, but they'll find you, if you make yourself findable and attractive as a source of advice.

BENJAMIN

How do I do that?!

PELOWITZ

This will be the key challenge you face over your career. In my judgment, you do this by successfully passing through three gates, proving you have the desire, ability and fortitude to achieve excellence in this profession.

There are so many reasons people want to become a financial advisor. The big one is the industry's high average compensation. But those figures distort the reality, as averages do. Some advisors do very well, and some do surprisingly poorly. That's why you have to pass through these three gates of excellence. You pass the first one after trying it out for a while and recognizing – not that you can do the job but that you *like* the job, or better yet, *love* the job. When you can honestly say "this is for me," "this is the way I can utilize my talents to make a unique contribution to the world," then you've passed through the first gate.

The ability to do the job takes more than just academic training, and more than just fluency with the market and comfort with numbers. It takes experience working with people, understanding their goals, their personalities and their challenges, and helping them pave a path to greater financial security. When you've spent a year forging relationships with flesh-and-blood clients and come to see financial advice as less the science of quantitative optimization and more of a people profession, you've passed the second gate.

The third gate is the most challenging of all. This is the one they don't tell you about in advisor training. They are going to teach you how to build a book of business: through building teams, getting referrals, devising an elevator speech, using social media, handling objections on fees and constantly feeding your pipeline of prospective clients. The point of all this is to "grow your business," but they omit how *you* grow as a person, which I would argue is of greater importance to your long-term success. They'll never say this and it's just not part of the business lexicon. However, my many decades in the business tell me one thing: You can't manipulate your way to business success. But you *can* attract prospects and clients by becoming the sort of person they want on their side. You pass through that third gate by acquiring wisdom and developing character.

BENJAMIN

How will I know I have done that?

PELOWITZ

When you're known as an excellent advisor.

SCENE 3

BENJAMIN, REGGIE and SOPHIE are standing at the counter of a Century City coffee shop, awaiting their drinks.

BARISTA

Apricot Ceylon tea latte for Sophie – at the counter.

Sophie looks up from her phone and moves to the counter. Benjamin perks up and steps towards her.

BENJAMIN

Excuse me, are you by chance the Sophie who hates sales?

SOPHIE

Uh, what?

BENJAMIN

Joseph Pelowitz tells me I have a kindred spirit at the Tilden Prescott training.

SOPHIE

Ah, yes, guilty as charged.

BARISTA

Double espresso for Reggie? Small mocha for Benjamin?

Reggie grabs the drinks for them both.

BENJAMIN

Hi, I'm Benjamin Pearl and this is my friend Reggie Gleam.

SOPHIE

Nice to meet you both. I'm taking my drink with me. Are you as well, or are you taking a seat?

REGGIE

No, we're also heading over to the training.

They go out the door and walk down the street together.

The two of you have a lot of guts taking on a job based on selling if you say you hate sales.

SOPHIE

I choose not to see the job as selling. If that's how I saw it, I simply couldn't do it. I look at it this way: There are people out there who want to invest their capital, and are looking for a partner willing to invest her knowledge and effort. I call that collaboration, not sales.

BENJAMIN

Wow. I think I'm going to memorize that line.

REGGIE

I for one hope to become recognized as a collaboration leader. Who is this Pelowitz fellow you both know?

SOPHIE

My parents have been clients of his for decades.

BENJAMIN

He's a friend of my dad's from the neighborhood. I met with him yesterday to get his advice.

REGGIE

Interesting, because I'm not familiar with his name. I searched every list I could find of the top advisors in L.A., ranked by assets under management. Robert Stephenson, a Tilden Prescott advisor down in the Miracle Mile, topped the list. We met yesterday afternoon, and he offered a lot of pointers. We should definitely compare notes.

BENJAMIN

Mr. Pelowitz offered me tremendous reassurance. He basically said that success in this business comes down to three things. First is seeing your work as a vocation, as a means of making a unique contribution to the world. Second is seeing your clients qualitatively rather than quantitatively, which means understanding the goals, personalities and challenges behind the numbers. And third is acquiring wisdom and developing your own character, becoming the sort of person clients will profit from associating with.

REGGIE

Those are nice general guidelines, but how do you implement them? Robert Stephenson offered a lot of concrete advice on how he got to where he is, managing over $6 billion in client assets. And to be honest, much of what he said sounded kind of opposite to what Pelowitz says, and quite a bit more compelling. He said you've got to run your practice like a business, which means paying close attention to the numbers.

Beyond the first three years or so, where all efforts are geared to building an advisory practice, the name of the game becomes how you can constantly fuel the growth of your business, and reach the standard of living you want and need personally and which will ultimately serve your clients as you upgrade the business. The first key number he said is 2,000. You've got about 2,000 hours a year to devote to your business, so you need to think carefully about how you allocate that time. His cardinal rule is that most of that time should go to new prospects. Using up your time on existing clients will inhibit future growth.

Dealing with your current client base is of course important, but even there you need to do so wisely. First, you hire new trainees such as ourselves to handle most of these relationships. Stephenson recommends segmenting your book of business, dividing it into A-clients, B-clients and C-clients.

The A-clients are the ones who most actively contribute to the growth of your business. These are the ones you should be calling and meeting with. Your staff handles the B-clients, with a view toward moving them up to the A-category or confirming them as C-clients, who are encouraged to find a more suitable advisor.

SOPHIE

That sounds horrendous! And how could you convert a B-client to an A- or C-client anyway? The client's intermediate level of revenue is apparently what categorizes him as B.

REGGIE

Stephenson's got an ingenious system. He's got software that breaks down how much each client generates in annual revenue, and how much time that client took from your 2,000 hours a year. And he grades clients on how effective they have been as referral sources.

BENJAMIN

Sounds like the client is working for the advisor, and not the other way around.

SOPHIE

It also sounds like the clients who helped Stephenson get to where he is when he was a rookie like us are the ones he's throwing under the bus. He was all too happy to take on that C-client when he was just starting out, but now that he's the firm's top producer, they are apparently draining him of his precious time.

REGGIE

You're looking at this as more sinister than it actually is. Stephenson says business is all about mutual benefit. He hosts a lavish party at his Bel Air mansion every year for his best clients and referral sources. He wants to thank them for their contribution to his business and to encourage further contributions. But businesses are dynamic entities. Sometimes former business collaborators are no longer suited to each other, so they go their separate ways, amicably.

BENJAMIN

As a consumer, I don't want my advisor's thanks. If I hire a lawyer, I want him to win the case for me, not to apportion some of the hours he billed me to a banquet at his home.

REGGIE

Benjamin, I think you live in a nice home in a nice neighborhood – similar to mine. But with all due respect, you said Pelowitz lives in your area. Well, Beverlywood is not Bel Air. He's done well, but he's not reached the same level of success as Robert Stephenson has. Everyone on the top advisor list I looked at managed at least $1 billion. Pelowitz was nowhere on that list. And Stephenson's extreme level of wealth was no barrier to his taking the time to speak with me as Pelowitz did with you.

They arrive at Tilden Prescott offices for advisor training.

Looks like we'll need to continue this another time. They're opening the doors for our first session.

ACT II

SCENE 1

First day of training commences at Tilden Prescott's Century City Offices, where 30 new recruits hear Mark Macher explain the difference between good ideas and good business.

MACHER

Okay, team: Today's session will be devoted primarily to building a book of business. We'll also talk a little bit at the end of our session about segmenting that book on the basis of revenue. That's not something rookies need to worry about, but everyone should have a sense of the end goal.

Each of you has been paired with one of our local advisor teams each afternoon to get a sense of the day-to-day operations of an advisory firm. There you'll get a feel for how we interact with clients. But our morning sessions will be devoted to how you get clients. Because unless you can do that, you're not going to make it in this business – as we discussed.

Now, the path to acquiring clients may look different for each of you on a superficial level. Some of you will turn to your friends and neighbors; others will find them by serving on a board of directors for a local charity. And still others will create your own networking events. But regardless of the venue or client type, the process will be the same:

First, you broadcast a clear value proposition; second, you build a network around a defined target group; and third, you engage prospects and motivate them to take action.

Now, let me hear from *you*. Give me an example, somebody, of your value proposition.

TRAINEE 1

"We provide our clients financial peace of mind."

MACHER

That doesn't work. It's too general. Why should I hand over my hard-earned savings to you instead of the hundreds of others also undoubtedly offering financial peace of mind. A value proposition needs to be unique. Anybody else?

BENJAMIN

proudly...

"We help you identify your goals and keep your spending, savings, debt management and insurance needs on track. We advise on estate planning and beneficiary documents, as well as investments. We monitor your progress on each of these items at our annual meetings, or more frequently if you prefer, and our guidance for needed changes is highly specific."

MACHER

Not horrible. It's an interesting list of services. But it's missing a key element, actually two key elements, but one of them is so vital that without it, I can't really respect this value proposition. Can anybody fix our biggest deficiency?

REGGIE

Yeah. Instead of saying "We help you identify your goals..." at the beginning, it should say "We help professional entertainers identify their goals..." or "We help wine enthusiasts identify their goals..." It's missing the niche.

And it's also missing a call to action at the end, like "Is this relevant to you?" or "Basically, we're here to help people like you become wealthy."

MACHER

What's your name?!

REGGIE

Reggie Gleam.

MACHER

You are going to shine as a wealth manager. That is my prediction, Gleam. You got it *exactly* right.

BENJAMIN

With all due respect, Mr. Macher, and with sincere appreciation for my friend Reggie's enhancement of my value proposition, I'm bothered by this. I can see how under certain circumstances it would be beneficial to add Reggie's suggested words. But inserting words such as "wine enthusiasts" seems to me to be of secondary importance. And the last bit – "Is this relevant to you?" – feels a bit pushy to me.

My suggested value proposition, which I have actually put a lot of thought into prior to today's session, is highly substantive. I asked myself what I would want if I were seeking this service, and my answer was a detailed list of specialized services accompanied by generous support. I mean, that's really what people need and want, right? Genuine expertise and professional handholding.

MACHER

What's *your* name?

BENJAMIN

Benjamin Pearl.

MACHER

We'll need to extract you from your oyster before your light is ready to shine, Pearl.

Look, we accepted you into this program for a reason, so you obviously have the potential to succeed. But you really need to learn, and sooner rather than later, that ideas are a dime a dozen. Business requires selling. You can have the greatest value prop in the world, but most people, most of the time, need to be reassured that what you're talking about relates to them.

And another thing: Time is money. It's not enough to motivate one person to take action when you can at the same time fill your pipeline with several potential clients. That's why Reggie's answer was spot on. He added both of our two missing elements. By including a niche, he made your value proposition, which was unique – I give you credit for that – referable. By asking if it was relevant to the person he was speaking with, he queued up his prospect to take an action. After all, a film industry exec is generally *proud* to be a film industry exec. Rejecting a pitch like that is almost like shunning his identity.

Okay, team. Here's your homework for this week. Write this down.

First, I want you to define your niche – the target group you are seeking as clients. Second, you need to develop a value proposition that is unique, referable and actionable. Third, I want you to memorize that value proposition – at least a shortened version of it. This is what we call an "elevator speech" – something you can confidently say to someone you meet on an elevator before you reach the ground floor. Fourth, I want you to create a brochure based on your value proposition that you can use as text for your websites. Fifth, I am e-mailing to each of you a modifiable sales script that you can customize based on your unique niches and value propositions.

Oh, and one more thing. I wouldn't wait too long before getting this all together and beginning your networking. We will be tracking your progress on a weekly basis. Besides helping out in your advisor partners' offices, you will begin building your own businesses immediately.

SCENE 2

STEPHENSON explains his approach to REGGIE in their Miracle Mile office.

STEPHENSON

In the middle of their conversation...

I can say it in a single word, Reggie: "Outsourcing." That is *the* most useful business model for a financial advisor. There simply isn't enough time to do everything it takes to service clients. Nor is there any need or benefit to reinvent the wheel. There are others out there who can do it better and cheaper than you could.

REGGIE

I feel privileged to be assigned to your office as a trainee. So, first of all, what should I *not* being doing?

STEPHENSON

The list of what not to do is a mile long. It includes researching investments, making changes to client portfolios, monitoring portfolios on an ongoing basis, developing financial plans, setting up and monitoring small business retirement plans, sending out...

REGGIE

Proudly...

I think I get it. I need to focus my time on client-facing activities exclusively, figuring out how to answer their personal concerns, offering high-touch customer service and the like, right?

STEPHENSON

That's what a lot of advisors think, and there was a time when that was the norm for top advisors. But that won't cut it anymore. If you want to reach the *very* top, than you need stay focused on productive activities exclusively. There's plenty of technological solutions nowadays to handle client communications better than you could.

We use a platform that enables us to have custom-tailored personal conversations with clients and prospects based on their e-mail, voice-mail or text-message queries. You don't waste your time crafting a lengthy financial plan. You just open the program, enter a keyword and you gain instant access to customizable guidebooks, infographics and thought leadership, all of it segmented into a variety of customer personas, with embedded analytics to measure the recipient's engagement.

REGGIE

Whoa! That's really cool! So what *should* I be focusing on?

STEPHENSON

Just one thing: You are an asset gatherer. That is your primary occupation. The beauty of the software I was just describing goes far beyond its curated content. As you familiarize yourself with its capabilities, you will see that every communication serves as information requested by the client or prospect and simultaneously as a marketing campaign. It allows you to relate to the client on a very deep level, to have these personal conversations, while at the same time deploying targeted lead-generation campaigns to uncover new assets and generate fresh referrals. This outsourced solution toolifies every aspect of advisor-client interactions to speed up results, increase client satisfaction and differentiate us from our competitors. With the click of a few buttons, it motivates prospects to take action while nurturing our existing relationships – all without having to devote the time and expense of building these capabilities from scratch.

REGGIE

This just blows my mind. I can't wait to get started. This is so different from what my friend Benjamin is doing at Joseph Pelowitz's office.

STEPHENSON

The old advisory service model had its role in the 20th century, but it doesn't meet the needs of today's consumers. I think the relative size of my business and Pelowitz's makes a pretty clear statement about which model is more effective.

SCENE 3

> PELOWITZ explains his approach to BENJAMIN in their Wilshire Blvd. office and takes a call from SOPHIE.

PELOWITZ

On the phone, with Benjamin seated in front of him.

Hi Sophie. Nice to hear from you. How is Miami treating you? *(pause)* Ahh, yes, Bal Harbour. So you're at our Collins Avenue branch. I know that's close to your grandmother. How wonderful. Look, I've got my new trainee Benjamin Pearl sitting in with me now. Can you call me back in half an hour? Terrific. Talk with you then. *(pause)* I certainly will.

Apologies for the delay, Benjamin. Your fellow trainee, Sophie Mandel, sends her warm personal regards.

BENJAMIN

Please return mine to her. I was wondering what became of her.

PELOWITZ

Her parents have been clients of mine for about 20 years. Her father, Michael Mandel, informed me that his mother has been declining in her ability to function independently and lives alone in Sunny Isles Beach. Since she was unwilling to move to L.A., Sophie was in a bind. She is extremely devoted to her grandmother and wanted to be there to help, but was worried that meant putting her career on hold. I told them that we have offices in South Florida as well, and since her particular area of interest is in retirement planning, there's probably no better place in the U.S. to start building such a practice. She was also concerned that L.A. is where she prefers to be long-term. But nowadays state borders are hardly a barrier to conducting business; she can get licensed in both states. My only caution was that she ought to disclose to prospective clients that the day could come when she might open an office in L.A. and be based out here, making regular visits to Miami of course. She was thrilled. We're set to discuss her first client retirement plan this afternoon.

BENJAMIN

She's clearly a very caring person. I'm glad to hear that people like her are not excluded from this business. Apropos of which, I wanted to make sure I'm not excluded from this business either, for a different reason. I was hoping you could help me clarify something I learned in Macher's advisor training session.

PELOWITZ

Sure thing.

BENJAMIN

I proposed what I thought was a very solid value proposition, and Macher could not endorse it until my friend Reggie inserted two seemingly minor additions. Now, I have no ego investment in this. My concern was that the two additions felt to me to be cheapening my value proposition, which was very substantive, by inserting vaporous appeals to wine enthusiasts and sales pressure pushing for a decision.

PELOWITZ

Sighs...

I hear your frustration, Benjamin. You want to be authentic, and you feel that the thrust of the training they're giving you is to make you robotic.

BENJAMIN

Exactly!

PELOWITZ

I get it. But, without being robotic, you need to strike a balance between what makes good business sense and what you're comfortable with. The business development wonks have turned sales – or think they've turned sales – into a science. They've measured and tested the sales process *ad nauseam*. They're so confident in their findings, and so distrustful of the weakness of the human beings they employ as financial advisors, that they've turned everything into platforms and tools meant to tickle the part of the human brain thought responsible for releasing all of their hard-earned money to the person requesting it. But technology cannot penetrate the subtlety of authentic human interaction.

Overall, having a business niche makes some sense. Determining a comfortable way to help your interlocutor commit to an investment program rather than defer the matter indefinitely is also an important part of doing business. So you can screen out what you find absurd and you can adapt ideas that need to be filtered through your own innate way of relating to the world.

In short, if you adopt wholesale everything they tell you to do, you're a robot. If you dismiss it all, you're agoraphobically hiding inside your comfort zone.

Phone rings...

Ahh. Sophie's calling me back.

BENJAMIN

This has been a great help, Mr. Pelowitz. Thank you so much!

Leaves...

PELOWITZ

Picks up phone...

Perfect timing, Sophie. Thank you for calling me back. Benjamin sends his warm regards, by the way. Just to let you know, I've got another meeting in half an hour, but you've got my full attention until then. How can I help you?

SOPHIE

Thank you so much for allowing me this time. I just wanted to get your input on how I should approach retirement investing as I engage the mostly younger people I am in contact with. For a lot of them, the subject seems so remote because it is so far off in time, and yet as you and I know, there's no better time to start preparing for it than when you've got a long time horizon ahead of you.

PELOWITZ

Great question, Sophie. And let me first say that I think you're absolutely right to focus on your age-peers. You'll have more credibility with this group, and the "supply" as it were of unadvised people in this demographic is ample. But to your question, I would say that the first thing you need to do is make it real for them. You can't easily talk with a 21-year-old about being 71. That's half a century a way, and they haven't seen even half that amount of time in their lives. So the first thing to do is break it down for them in way that is digestible. Start off by telling them they can look at their life divided into thirds. That is within everybody's ability to conceptualize. They may even initially grasp this as work-time, free-time and sleep-time. But you'll clarify that what you're really getting at is the reality that most people nowadays, whether voluntarily or involuntarily, are not working during that last third of their lives.

SOPHIE

Or put differently, I could say that in the first segment of their lives, their parents support them; in the second, they're supporting themselves; and their support in the third segment comes from what they supply in the segment they're currently in.

PELOWITZ

That's a very meaningful way of starting this thought process, Sophie.

The next step would be to explain that in order to avoid a serious problem in that final third of their lives, they need two things: They need income, and they need assets. Ideally, with their parents' encouragement, young people should begin thinking about this before they graduate high school, which is when I had a similar talk with you and your parents, if you recall.

SOPHIE

I certainly do. You gave us some eye-popping number for the average amount of student loan debt, and that encouraged me to work hard to get a scholarship. You also offered several ideas as to how to make it through college without any loans, whether that meant community college, an online program or even an overseas program. I want you to know that some of the acceptances I received, I joyfully crossed off my list – including some prestigious ones – because of their prohibitive costs. And I left college without a trace of debt.

PELOWITZ

Nothing could be more pleasing to the ears of a financial advisor than to remove negative income from a client's balance sheet. So now we can address positive income, and assets. And here's the key thing, Sophie. People need to make astute trades. I'm definitely not talking about trading stocks, which is usually a losing proposition. Rather, I'm talking about trading what is of lesser value for what is of greater value.

For example, a young college grad earning $48,000, without student loan debt and unmarried, can sock away, say, half his money in an investment. If our young professional can put away $24,000 for a period of 40 years at, say, a rate of 7% a year, he'll have nearly $5 million awaiting him at the other end.

SOPHIE

This is exactly why I wanted to have this talk, because the doubt that arises here is the trade-off that my peers typically feel regarding saving for retirement versus buying a home. One comes at the expense of the other. How do we balance that?

PELOWITZ

That is a key question, and the answer will differ depending on the client's individual situation. That's why advice needs to be personalized and not spewed out of a computerized financial plan. Your clients may include young singles and young marrieds. Their needs and expectations will differ. But in general terms, all should be looking to build their incomes, through career advancement, and build assets that grow in value over time.

So let's say a lovely young lady seized the opportunity afforded by her debt-free college graduation and high-paying initial salary to get that retirement ball rolling.

SOPHIE

I'm trying.

PELOWITZ

As I knew you were. And let's say you marry and start a family in the next few years.

SOPHIE

I'm working on that as well.

PELOWITZ

I'm sure you will succeed at both. So at some point you may want to plow the income you're diverting from your salary to saving up for a home – minus the funds you continue to use to max out on your workplace retirement plan, of course. You then buy a suitable home, financed with a mortgage. As time goes on you'll end up paying off more principal than interest, and eventually you'll have a completely paid off asset.

SOPHIE

That sounds highly appealing, probably to most people. And yet there are those who say that you're shortchanging yourself because stocks have higher average returns than real estate. Or that real estate ownership entails the high costs of mortgage interest, property taxes and home maintenance.

PELOWITZ

That is what many people say, but I don't think there is, or can be, any conclusive evidence of this. All of the data is inherently backward-looking and is all based on averages. You're well aware of just how rewarding it has been to be owners of real estate in our part of L.A. I'm not saying that real estate is better than stocks. Again, it comes down to the client's personal situation. Buying too much home can shortchange your stock portfolio. But in some cases – such as those blessed with large families – too little home isn't ideal either. Again, in general terms, whether you're married with two kids, married with four kids or single, one of your financial goals should be becoming an owner of assets that appreciate over time. One advantage of this – getting back to that final third of life where career income has ended – is that the assets provide a buffer against expenditure shocks. Right? If your home is paid off, that means you no longer need to pay rent. If somebody needs expensive prescription drugs – which has been known to happen late in life – their owned assets help them to buffer the shock of these expenses. So you're right about mortgage interest, property taxes and home maintenance, but neither can you live inside of your stocks rent free.

SOPHIE

It's really refreshing to hear you say this because – excuse me for my bluntness – there seems to be a bias towards stocks connected to the fact that advisors are compensated on the basis of the portfolios they manage, which include stocks but exclude real estate.

PELOWITZ

Unfortunately, that bias does exist. It's not because financial advisors are any greedier than other professionals. It's just human nature. Self-interest blinds people. But the best thing an advisor can do is see their clients as multi-dimensionally as they are, and not pretend they don't have needs and interests outside of investment securities. For most people, that includes home ownership. If you're not giving them objective advice, then what's the point?

SOPHIE

So objectively speaking, what is the point I should be communicating to my peers to open up these discussions about building their income and assets?

PELOWITZ

Let them know that it's all about making good trades – not trading stocks or flipping homes – but trading their human capital for the compensation they receive through their work, and trading their present consumption for future consumption. Developing one's career, limiting one's discretionary spending, but buying stocks of public companies and a home to live in and eventually own are good trades. The best trade – the one that can buy your clients retirement security, is trading the short-term for the long-term.

Looks like my meeting will begin shortly. I hope I helped answer your questions, Sophie. Please keep me posted on your progress.

SOPHIE

I can't thank you enough, Mr. Pelowitz. You've given me a lot to think about, and to start doing.

ACT III

SCENE 1

REGGIE begins his prospecting campaign at Constellation Place, a Century City office building filled with his target clients.

REGGIE, dressed in an expensive suit, approaches building's security guard.

GUARD

Who are you here to see today, sir?

REGGIE

I'm here to meet with some prospective clients.

GUARD

Okay. Which office would that be?

REGGIE

The elevator.

GUARD

Come again?

REGGIE

I know this sounds strange (*reading his badge*)…Charlie. Let me explain. Here's my card. I'm a financial advisor with Tilden Prescott in the Miracle Mile. We also have a large branch in the next office building over, as you may know. Our firm addresses the unique wealth management concerns of entertainment industry professionals. Our client roster includes actors, producers, directors, writers, managers and agents, and my job is to introduce these artists and creators to the capabilities we offer in the areas of..."

GUARD

Abruptly...before turning to a driver delivering a package.

Hold on (*glancing at the card*)...Reginald.

Turning to the driver...

Is that for the Digital Media Group? Yes, they're expecting that. You can leave it with me and I'll sign....Thanks.

Turning back to REGGIE.

It doesn't sound to me like you work in this building, Reginald. I'm a little preoccupied. Can you state your business here, or come back at another time?

REGGIE

Taking off his watch and placing it before the guard.

I can see you're busy and I'll get right to the point. I'm putting my trusty Seiko mechanical diver's watch in front of you. You can time me. If I'm not back here before one hour is up, I forfeit the watch. You can also see me at all times through your security monitor. I'll be in or just outside the elevator the whole time. Here's the point. I've done my research. Your building, Charlie, is *the* best place for our firm in all of L.A. Where else can I find several talent agencies, entertainment lawyers and business managers all in one spot, and with 35 floors to talk with the artists coming to visit them? Please, Charlie – I've put down my watch, here's my driver's license and I'll think of some way to repay your kindness. And like I said, you'll see me every second on your screen. But I've got to perform for my firm and I know of no better way to succeed at my job than to spend an hour each day riding your elevator.

GUARD

You've got me in an unusually good mood right now, Reginald. If I see you wander off during any of this time, I'll have you arrested. I'll give you a shot at this, with no promises about the future. Good luck.

REGGIE

You're a prince. I won't let you down. And I go by Reggie, by the way. Thank you!

> *Slips on a Rolex. Waits by the elevators. Two open up. Chooses the elevator that only one other person enters, a woman who pushes floor 24. REGGIE pushes 35. Doors close.*

If I'm not mistaken, those are 10-millimeter Japanese Akoya pearls. Their unparalleled luster give them away.

FEMALE PASSENGER 1

Disconcerted...

Could be. That sounds about right. I'm not sure – my husband bought me this necklace.

REGGIE

Your husband has exquisite taste.

Actively pauses, to encourage her response.

FEMALE PASSENGER 1

Discombobulated.

Are you a jeweler or something?

REGGIE

No. Well, in a weird way...yes. I'm a financial advisor at Tilden Prescott working with entertainment industry professionals, including actors, producers, directors, writers, managers and agents, and discussions around jewelry are an everyday occurrence with this bunch.

Door opens.

Here's my card if you or your husband fit our client demographic and are ever looking for financial – or jewelry – advice.

FEMALE PASSENGER 1, creeped out, takes card and tosses it after elevator closes. Elevator opens again on 35th floor. Man enters and presses Lobby.

MALE PASSENGER 1

Did you want to get out?

REGGIE

No, no. Looks like I've arrived here too early, but thanks so much.

Passenger smiles. REGGIE breaks the elevator silence.

If I'm not mistaken, from this distance, that appears to be a Breguet Marine watch.

MALE PASSENGER 1

No. This is a Raymond Weil Shine I got from my dad.

REGGIE

Sweet. Do you like it?

MALE PASSENGER 1

Love it, man. Tells me the time whenever I want to know it. Are you a watch collector or something?

REGGIE

No. Well, in a weird way…yes. I'm a financial advisor at Tilden Prescott working with entertainment industry professionals, including actors, producers, directors, writers, managers and agents, and discussions around watches are an everyday occurrence with this bunch.

MALE PASSENGER 1

Cool. I'm an actor. You have a card or something? Financial advice could come in handy at some point.

Door opens.

REGGIE

Sure. Here are a few. Please let your entertainment industry colleagues know about our service as well. Could I take your number? I'm unavailable at the moment, but would be happy to give you a call later today.

MALE PASSENGER 1

Sure thing. My name's Rod.

They exchange information.

REGGIE

How serendipitous that we met in an elevator like this. I'll give you a call this afternoon, Rod.

MALE PASSENGER 1 (ROD)

Okay, dude.

REGGIE looks at his watch and eyes an area opposite to where ROD is heading. Each is now out of the other's view. REGGIE pushes the up button and enters with MALE PASSENGER 2.

Wow – a Cartier watch and Charvet tie! Are you a graduate of the Sorbonne?

MALE PASSENGER 2

Taken aback.

I've never been to France. And if I have no clue who made this tie, how could you possibly know?

REGGIE

The artisanal handwoven fabric and unique shimmer seemed to be dead giveaways. But I could be mistaken. I'm not a tailor, but as a financial advisor whose clientele tend to dress expensively, I've learned a thing or two about fashion accessory brands.

MALE PASSENGER 2

Ahh, so you're a financial advisor! I'd be very interested to know what you do to make the estate-planning issues related to the death of your client's spouse easier for those handling the distribution of assets.

REGGIE

Flummoxed...

Umm, well, er, our platform offers sophisticated solutions custom-tailored to the unique needs of ultra-high-net-worth clients seeking...um...solutions to their estate-planning distribution needs. We...that is our team of advisors, have access to Tilden Prescott's specialists – technical specialists in the field – who, um, manage distributions tax-efficiently to, er, optimize after-tax income...

Doors open.

I'd be happy to discuss this with you in greater detail later if you'd like. Here's my card.

MALE PASSENGER 2

Rebuffs the card...

Look, I collaborate with financial advisors on these issues all the time. I'm sorry to say, but your answer did not inspire confidence. My advice to you is to spend less time on shimmering neckties and more time on substance. As an estate-planning attorney, my job is to provide advanced planning around transferring wealth so as to avoid potential conflict among remaining family members, minimize estate tax and preserve clients' wealth for many generations. This is a very sensitive and consequential business matter!

> *MALE PASSENGER 2 leaves while FEMALE PASSENGER 2 enters, door shuts.*

REGGIE

Am I right that that is a Hermes watch?

FEMALE PASSENGER 2

It is indeed. The lettering isn't that big. You must have very good eyes.

REGGIE

Nah. It's kind of an occupational hazard. Our clients at Tilden Prescott Wealth Management tend to sport attractive accessories and, among them, watches in particular resonate with me as a metaphor for the passage of time and building of a legacy.

FEMALE PASSENGER 2

That's great if your *clients* are building a legacy, but what does that have to do with their *advisors*?

REGGIE

You're right. Our clients are high achievers in the entertainment and related industries. *They're* the ones with the vision, but their advisors' job is to handle the advanced planning around transferring wealth so as to avoid potential conflicts among family members, minimize estate tax and preserve clients' wealth for many generations.

FEMALE PASSENGER 2

Sounds like a cross between psychologist and CPA.

REGGIE

It's a sensitive and consequential business matter, and we therefore work closely with the clients' tax professionals, estate attorney or other trusted advisors on a continual basis – people like the attorney with the shimmering tie I was talking with as you got on.

> *Doors open. REGGIE and FEMALE PASSENGER 2 exit together...*

FEMALE PASSENGER 2

Oh yeah. You mean Kenneth Kuang. He's one of the top trust attorneys in L.A.

REGGIE

There's enough talent resident in this one building to change the world!

If you happen to be in entertainment or a related profession, take my card and feel free to contact me if our firm's capabilities can ever be of value to you or other professionals like yourself.

> *FEMALE PASSENGER 2 takes card and heads in one direction, while REGGIE heads to GUARD.*

Hello Charlie. Thank you again for giving me a shot. I think I did pretty well for a first day, except for one thing. I arrived here about half a minute after the appointed time. I forfeit my diver's watch.

GUARD

Take the watch, Reggie.

REGGIE

I won't make it in this business if I don't maintain discipline. That means rewarding myself when I do well, and penalizing myself when I mess up. So I can't allow myself to take back that watch. With your permission, though, may I take another elevator ride the same time tomorrow?

GUARD

See you tomorrow. Good luck.

REGGIE smiles and leaves.

SCENE 2

Three months later, Tilden Prescott Rookies graduate at a ceremony in the firm's Century City offices

MACHER

I want to congratulate all of you who made it to our graduation. You are all achievers. You are all highly competitive. The proof of that is that 15 of you are present where 30 of you sat just three months ago. Everyone here is truly top-of-class.

You know by now that I have been nothing if not honest with you. By the end of three years, nearly half of this graduation class will likely survive in this business, but not with Tilden Prescott. Only the best of you will have the golden opportunity to call on prospects as a representative of Tilden Prescott than as a representative of Joe Blow Wealth Management.

As an incentive to keep at it, we have some graduation gifts for all of you, including some elegant bull and bear cufflinks or earrings, Tiffany & Co. money clips and his and hers Gucci leather case to use when handing out your business cards – all embossed with the name Tilden Prescott. But in addition to this, which all of you get, we also have our top producer award for just one of you. Get used to this. Tilden Prescott is a meritocracy, and we accord our best advisors with the treatment they deserve. So, for a weeklong all-expenses paid visit to the Waikiki Beach Resort, including first-class travel, free golf, snorkeling, car rental and gourmet food including an authentic Hawaiian luau [*drumroll*] I invite to the podium the Tilden Prescott rookie-advisor top producer…Reggie Gleam!

REGGIE

Wow, thank you Mark. This is quite a surprise, and an honor. I am really very humbled by this recognition, and by the extremely generous gift. I've worked very hard to build a book of business, and I can tell you all quite honestly, that I'd never have gotten as far as I have without the constant advice, help and support of my mentor Robert Stephenson, with whom I have been working as a junior advisor these past three months. I don't know if this is within protocol or not, but maybe the best way I can say thank you to Tilden Prescott, to Robert Stephenson and to my friends in this group would be to invite Robert to come up and offer you all a bit of his insight on how he became the top financial advisor in Los Angeles. Would that be okay, Mark?

Away from the mic, MACHER heartily agrees. REGGIE turns to STEPHENSON.

Robert...

Takes the podium.

STEPHENSON

Can we have a big round of applause for Stephenson Wealth Management's outgoing junior account executive and incoming vice president, Reggie Gleam!

Applause.

And thanks also to my friend Mark Macher for yielding the podium. Mark and I go back a long way. We were college basketball teammates when Mark first recruited me for this position, and I took seriously his charge to me to develop a winning team here at Tilden Prescott. And Reggie will soon be off to Hawaii because he took seriously my charge to him to win over new client assets, and I think all of you seated here today can do the same, if you've got that same drive to succeed that Reggie has. And if you don't, then *why* don't you?

If your team is well managed, you have no choice but to succeed. You know why? Because in a well-managed team everybody knows what he or she is there to do at every part of the day. Some of my fellow Tilden Prescott colleagues have been known to call our firm a jock shop. That's a bit of an exaggeration – a few of our associates come from that same basketball team that Mark Macher recruited me from, and some of our younger execs come from later generations of that same team, or other teams, but we've got some non-athletes too, and they're just as driven as the rest of us. We hire them because of their training, knowledge and work ethic, and we manage them to succeed.

Like Reggie, I too won Tilden Prescott's trainee top producer trip to Hawaii more years ago than I care to acknowledge. And even though I had an incredible time on the beach and on the links, I'll share with you the most incredible experience I had there. I and my wife at the time found a cozy spot to enjoy our luau. When I got up to throw away something in the garbage a few feet away, I noticed a small piece of Polynesian chicken being carted away by a colony of ants. I couldn't stop watching this scene. There I saw a nugget of teriyaki chicken being lifted by a bunch of ants. I checked this folks. A single chicken nugget weighs about 16 grams. One of those ants weighs about 1 milligram. So that nugget was 16,000 times heavier than one of those ants. How would you feel about lifting something 16,000 times heavier than you? Yet those ants did it because of their incredible teamwork.

You know some people look down on ants. They're tiny; they're six feet below your eyeballs. I look up to them. Look at their productivity. Look at their cooperation. They suffer no doubts about what they should be doing at all times. And that's how I try to manage my team. Everyone knows their goals and everyone knows how they have performed against those goals in each quarter. Everyone knows how long to hold the ball, when to pass it, how to cooperate with each other team member.

By the way, let me tell you what our No. 1 goal is. We make money for our clients. That's right. We know where our bread is buttered, and we never forget the client. Just to give you one example, I've got one guy in our trading department who trades around client positions all day long. We're talking about penny-sized improvements in price, selling at upticks, buying back on downticks. But you know, it all adds up over time. And when our clients get their monthly performance reports, they can see they're getting real value for their fees.

Some folks call us a jock shop. I call us a sleek, well-honed instrument for achieving client financial goals. And I'm pleased to have Reggie Gleam on board to help us move that client ball forward. So congratulations again to all of you who have passed go in advisor training. And to you Reggie, I want to present something I give every new member of our team once they're hired for a permanent position: It's a large-folio, coffee-table pictorial book called "On The Job: How Ants Achieve Excellence."

REGGIE comes up to accept book.

REGGIE

I'm normally more interested in keeping ants *away* from my table, but based on what I have just learned from you, there's nothing I'm more eager to contemplate with my morning coffee, as I look forward to a productive day, than these little critters. Thank you Robert!

SCENE 3

BENJAMIN confers with PELOWITZ.

BENJAMIN

She's 30 years old and earns about $50,000 a year. She saves 5 percent of her gross income in her 401(k) plan and receives a dollar-for-dollar company match. Her company does not match employee contributions above 5 percent of income. We're estimating 7 percent annual returns on her stock ETFs, and we're factoring in her paying down her mortgage and maintaining a large liquidity fund, as you recommended to me, for emergency reserves and for opportunistic buying. Based on her individual health and family health history, we're including a longevity expectation of age 90. Her goal is to retire early at age 60 with a paid-off home, Social Security and $30,000 a year from her investment portfolio. It doesn't seem prudent, at this point, to factor anything more than a Social Security payment that is only 75 percent of the current payout, based on solvency concerns. Add in the current rate of health-care inflation, and it seems to me that she is underfunded. Here are my calculations on paper. Am I missing something or do these look right to you?

One particular concern of mine is that the prospective client – her name is Terri Calicott – also met with my friend Reggie Gleam for an initial consultation. She told me that Reggie said she is on track to achieve her goals. With her permission, I discussed the matter with Reggie, and he says they can get her to her goal with a portfolio 100% invested in stocks, which he would reduce to about 55% stocks when she reaches age 55. His numbers check out, and he faults us for the cash drag of our liquidity portfolio. What do you make of all this?

PELOWITZ

Glances at BENJAMIN's worksheet...

I think you handled this correctly, Benjamin. And I don't like Reggie's approach. Nowadays it's easy to click a button on an investment app and whip up the portfolio that will give you the percentage return you need to get the final numbers the client is looking for. But real life doesn't work quite as smoothly.

First of all, circumstances shift in two realms: in the client's life and at the macro level, and those two things tend to frustrate heroic return assumptions. Am I right to assume Terri is unmarried?

BENJAMIN nods affirmatively.

Okay, consider how things might change if she marries. The couple will have a dual income, and presumably growth-oriented careers that will bring about increasing income. They may then have children with all sorts of associated expenses, including possibly a bigger home than she's currently thinking about. On the macro level, the economy will go up and down; there could be one or more job losses, as well as recessions and stock market crashes. The paradox here is that the liquidity portfolio's cash-drag that Reggie's computer program shows as reducing her returns is precisely the item that will ensure she and her family can survive the volatility in their household budget, and can actually give them a significant return boost when asset values fall during downturns. The app wants aggressive; real life and experience suggests otherwise.

BENJAMIN

That's what I thought. But I admit that the fact that Reggie was ranked No. 1 out of 15 and I came out No. 15 out of 15 gave me reason to want to double-check my math and assumptions.

PELOWITZ

Your math and assumptions *are* faulty, Benjamin. You were ranked No. 15 out of *30*, not 15 out of 15. Give yourself some credit.

Also, this client would be at great risk were her advisor, Reggie, to keep her 100% invested in stocks until just five years prior to her projected retirement. To reach her goals securely, she would need to have a minimum of three years' income saved up to ensure she needn't have to make portfolio withdrawals during her initial retirement on the chance a market downturn occurs during those first few years. Under those circumstances, she'd be forced to sell at depressed values. In a sense, Reggie is gambling with Terri's future. The averages used by these apps make it all seem safe, but nobody gets an *average* retirement. They retire once and the money's got to be there for them.

BENJAMIN

In other words, what you're saying is that if the sequence of returns works out such that stock values decline near the beginning stages of Terri's retirement, then she and similarly situated Stephenson clients are going to take a hard fall.

PELOWITZ

They're falling already.

BENJAMIN

Huh? What do you mean they're already falling? The stock market's been going gangbusters year after year. In this environment, you'd have to try really hard to put together a losing portfolio. Who…what…is falling?

PELOWITZ

One of my clients, a lawyer named Michael Mandel – you know his daughter, Sophie – explained this idea quite nicely. Let's say Robert Stephenson takes Terri's expensive porcelain vase and throws it from the top of his roof. He will be liable for the damage he caused. But if Stephenson is sitting across the room and throws a basketball at that same expensive vase – I gather he knows how to aim a ball – and then I come along and grab the vase just on time, Stephenson has no liability, even though in another second his intended action would have utterly smashed the vase.

The point I'm trying to illuminate – and this is not an attack against Stephenson per se, it is an industrywide problem – is that Stephenson, like so many of his colleagues, and asset managers – are already objects in motion – downward motion. They're going to fall at some point, and the impact on some clients will be destructive. Look at the retirement target-date fund industry. These funds tend to be quite aggressively invested, even at the retirement target date, when one would expect them to be allocated to non-risky assets. Why? Because like Stephenson, their fund managers know that a high proportion of stocks will give the funds higher long-term returns, which will boost fund sales. Many fund owners will benefit from this. But it is known in advance that those shareholders who retire just as the market is falling and who must make withdrawals at depressed prices are going to get clobbered. They'll never make back those losses and may have to look for work at an advanced age, reduce their standard of living or both.

If you remove that vase – let's call that vase Terri Calicott – you can save it, or her, from undue risk. By all means she can invest aggressively through most of her working years. And if she builds up a safe-money fund for her initial retirement years, she can remain aggressively invested in her principal portfolio even at initial retirement. But just as a falling vase enjoys no immunity from the law of gravity, neither is a high-risk portfolio immune from financial gravity. Investors should take risk, because they need growth, but they also require stability and liquidity, and the industry as a whole remains heedless of excessive risk.

ACT IV

SCENE 1

BENJAMIN meets with TERRI in his office.

BENJAMIN

I've very carefully considered your early-retirement objective, savings pattern and your investments, and I've also taken the liberty of discussing the matter with a senior advisor I used to work for until starting my own office here at Tilden Prescott. I've come to the following conclusion: Your goal is unachievable unless you make much more significant contributions to your retirement fund.

TERRI

Yikes! Are you sure about that? As I mentioned to you previously, one of your colleagues thought I was right on track.

BENJAMIN

I know. Since you permitted me to do so, I also spoke with Reggie about it. His firm invests more aggressively than we do, but the issue goes beyond our approaches to risk. The real issue is your lifestyle. If things remain static – if you intend to never marry and start a family, if you will always remain in that same condo on Beverly Glenn and if your salary will slightly more than double by age 60, then it is possible that you are on track to achieve your goals without any changes. Does that scenario fit?

TERRI

Gosh, I certainly hope not. I'm in a serious relationship right now. The street noise I hear from my condo is not something I will tolerate for more than another year or two. And I hope I can continue to increase my earnings, but it's not likely going to happen at that rate – not at my present company at least. But assuming you're right that I need to increase my retirement savings, I honestly don't know how I would do that in my present circumstances. That's why I was attracted to Reggie's proposal to consider investing in a higher-return fund. As he put it, "let your money work harder for you."

BENJAMIN

Pension funds are going bust across the country because their return assumptions allow people to pretend that their money is working harder for them, while the liabilities these funds need to pay out live in a non-pretend world in which retirees make claims against the fund.

I would rather take a more conservative approach to our planning, and then be pleasantly surprised if returns end up surpassing expectations. But just remember: the apps that advisors use to project returns do not arise from knowledge of future returns, but a lot of guesswork.

TERRI

So what do you suggest I do?

BENJAMIN

Terri, in the year that just ended, you earned a 7 percent return on a portfolio that totaled $150,000 at the start of the year. So you made $10,500. That's a nice, healthy return. Maybe markets will only deliver a 5 percent return this year, or maybe minus-5 percent. We can't always make our money work for us on command in the stock market. But, let's say you get rid of that noisy condo in West L.A. Maybe you get married and move into a similar-sized property in Valley Village, which is about the same distance from your current job. You will have cut your housing expenses by $1,000 a month. Now you've saved $12,000, not just one year but every year. You can plow that $12,000 into your investment account, and you're now supercharging your retirement savings. Or maybe, combining your resources with your future husband, you keep the condo in West L.A. and rent it out, while paying down the mortgage and acquiring a valuable asset. Either way, by the time you get to retirement, you've made more money than you otherwise would, while learning to *require* less money than you otherwise would.

TERRI

Where do I sign up as a client, Benjamin? This is exactly the kind of advice I need.

BENJAMIN

Chuckles. Calls assistant on office intercom.

Stacy, can you please assist Terri with the new-client paperwork?

I appreciate your confidence, Terri, and I look forward to working with you to achieve all of your financial goals.

STACY

I'll be happy to help you, Terri. And Benjamin, Sophie Mandel is waiting in the reception area. Can I escort her in?

BENJAMIN

Yes, please!

> *Walks out with Stacy and Terri, and returns with Sophie.*

Well welcome back to sunny Southern California from sunny South Florida! Did you even notice a difference?

SOPHIE

The thermometer reading is about the same both here and there this whole week – low to mid-80s, typical for late May, but it feels at least 10 degrees hotter there because of the humidity. I'm not missing the weather there, and I really missed my family and friends here. But I'm so glad I could be with my grandmother in her final year. We were always very close.

BENJAMIN

May she be remembered for a blessing always.

SOPHIE

Thank you, Benjamin. I've had time to mourn her loss with my family, and I'm now sort of picking up the pieces of my life in Florida and moving them here. I built up a larger clientele than I ever could have expected in just one year. They're mostly our age and career- and retirement-focused. People think of Florida as populated mainly by retirees, and it is in the top 5 states ranked by median age, but there's no shortage of young people there and maybe because of all of the retirees, young people seem more focused on this issue there. So I've been very fortunate to build up this business.

And before I even arrived here, somehow the word got out, and I quickly received a surprising and apparently generous offer from the Robert Stephenson Group to acquire my practice as a retirement subdivision to be run jointly by me and Reggie. While weighing that offer, Joseph Pelowitz suggested I consider whether collaborating with your firm would be worth exploring as an alternative option as I put down business roots in L.A.

BENJAMIN

I really appreciate your considering my firm as a potential partner, Sophie. Mr. Pelowitz briefed me on some of the details. One thing I need to note right up front is that, so far at least, Reggie and I appear to be in different leagues from a production point of view. He remains far and away the most successful member of our trainee graduating class. While I left training with a 15 out of 30 ranking, I'm pleased to say I've gradually moved up over this past year. And according to Mr. Pelowitz, your assets under management are about halfway between Reggie's and mine.

What that means is that from a financial point of view, you're likely to get better terms from Reggie than I have the capacity to offer. But I believe there's a better cultural fit between my practice and yours, and I'd venture to make the case that that, ultimately, is more important for you and your clients than any immediate financial benefits of merging with The Stephenson Group. In fact, I'd be so brazen as to argue that you'd be doing them *and* you both a favor by spurning their offer.

SOPHIE

What makes you say that? I'd be really interested to hear.

BENJAMIN

Quite simply the biggest challenge any acquiring firm faces is client retention. If they leave everything in your hands, then they probably have little to worry about. But that's not what the Robert Stephenson Group does. My impression is that clients who are not sufficiently forthcoming with new assets and referrals are looked down upon. These are *your* relationships they are likely to be messing with, and I imagine that some number of them will leave. That will, by the way, diminish their perception of the value you personally bring to the firm, so there will be tension down the road unless you agree to stand at the exit and keep clients from leaving.

SOPHIE

You're definitely speaking to my heart. Reggie mainly talked up the financial aspects of a merger. The Stephenson Group is so highly esteemed by Tilden Prescott that it can leverage loans from the parent firm and pay a higher multiple on high-quality practices. But my business is still too young to be worth much anyway, and you've reminded me of the reasons it would be a poor home for my clients.

While I was waiting to join Reggie for our meeting, I was taken aback by a large photobook on his coffee table on how ants achieve excellence. I had forgotten all about it by the time I left, until he introduced me to one of the firm's partners, whose wall was adorned with images of ant super-colonies. To each his own of course. In my office I've got a photo of some beautiful gazelles next to a pond at sunset. But what are the odds of two people in the same office sharing this unusual taste?

BENJAMIN

I think it's more than just two people there who pay homage to the ant. But in any case, we don't have the same financing that The Stephenson Group can access, though we can rebate revenues stemming from your excess contribution to the firm for an interim period. We're growing very rapidly, and I expect we'll have similar sized books of business within the year.

But of this you can be sure: Your clients will be happy here; they will get sound advice and guidance. This is not just an investment firm, where we tweak the portfolio and maybe get a few extra basis points of return. We offer comprehensive financial advice, and we focus on relationships, with a view toward making each client better off than they'd be without our input and net of fees.

SOPHIE

This is exactly the kind of partnership that I want for my clients.

BENJAMIN

I'm so glad this is of interest. Please take all the time you need to think it over. Now, at the risk of ruining the whole thing, there's one thing that I wanted to ask when we first met, before you suddenly left. I'm looking to build not just my business, but my life. Now that I'm starting to earn a respectable living, I am looking to meet the right person. I was impressed with you when we first met, even more impressed with you when you left to be with your grandmother and impressed to see how your financial-planning practice mirrors your fine character. There's a really nice restaurant on Wilshire and Wetherly if you'd like to explore this other avenue too.

SOPHIE

I'd love to go out with you, Benjamin. I'm also looking to build my life, and I was also impressed when we first met a year ago.

BENJAMIN

Well, this has been my best business meeting – ever! See you tonight at 7:00?

SOPHIE

Can't wait.

SCENE 2

Three years after graduation, the market has crashed. BENJAMIN and REGGIE meet on the elevator on the 35th floor of Constellation Place.

REGGIE

Speaking with Female Passenger No. 3.

We believe that markets will recover, and will reward investors who apply strategies that successfully manage volatility.

Elevator door opens on the top floor. FEMALE PASSENGER No. 3 gets out.

FEMALE PASSENGER No. 3

I'm glad my diamond necklace gets the highest grade for clarity. My husband will be happy to know that. But investing in the stock market during this crisis has got to be the worst possible option for our money. Good luck, Reginald.

Hands back his card. BENJAMIN enters elevator.

REGGIE

Benjamin! Great to see you! What brings you here?

BENJAMIN

Great to see you, Reggie! Are you getting off on this floor?

REGGIE

No, no. Just had some meetings with some prospective clients. And you?

BENJAMIN

Just had a great meeting with Kenneth Kuang, a lawyer in this building. He brought me into a meeting with a client looking for help with wealth transfer and intergenerational planning issues. If all works out, God willing, I may soon have my biggest client yet.

REGGIE

That's incredible, man. I'm really happy for you. How are Sophie and the twins?

BENJAMIN

Healthy and happy, and expecting another child in the summer! How are you and Samantha?

REGGIE

Getting married in June! Hey, do you have time to grab a coffee with me downstairs? I'm meeting Robert Stephenson here for lunch soon, but I'd love to get your perspective on things, if you can spare the time.

BENJAMIN

Absolutely. Your double espresso is on me. It's been a long time.

> *REGGIE and BENJAMIN exit elevator and walk to café in the lobby. BENJAMIN orders their drinks.*
>
> *Speaking to REGGIE...*

So how are you managing during these volatile times?

REGGIE

It's been tough. We've lost a lot of business. Our portfolio performance isn't looking that bright for the time being, and clients are irritable, or worse. We get calls every day that are unpleasant. And we're working late every night trying our best to maintain these relationships. I'm not sleeping well. My new client acquisition has been nil. No one wants to talk with me, and it's getting somewhat discouraging.

BARISTA

Double espresso, small mocha.

> *REGGIE and BENJAMIN take their coffees.*

REGGIE

Benjamin, I'll put this very directly. I respect your intelligence and experience, so here's the thing. If someone dropped in from out of nowhere and observed us in the elevator, they'd be certain that you're the successful one between us. You had a successful meeting with an incredible referral source; I had just gotten my fourth rejection in an embarrassingly short amount of time.

And if someone were observing us over a period of time, they'd be even surer that you were the successful one. You got the girl. Amazingly, you acquired her practice even though we had the better offer. Pearl Planning and Wealth Management is thriving by any measure, even now during a market crash. And yet, here's the thing. The numbers say otherwise. Our business, even just my division within The Stephenson Group, is larger than yours, even now during this crash. I'm happy for you, I really am. But why does it feel like you're succeeding and I'm not, even though, objectively speaking, The Stephenson Group is still the top wealth management firm in L.A.?

BENJAMIN

Sounds like your perception of our relative performance is colored by your having a hard day, Reggie. Like you said, you've got the numbers on your side. But for my part, I'd definitely agree that we're thriving. And my getting the girl is not unrelated to this. In both cases, in initiating my relationship with Sophie and in establishing client portfolios, I take only calculated risks. Before asking her out the first time, I spoke with Mr. Pelowitz, who confirmed she was not seeing anyone, was marriage-minded and, knowing both of us, thought we were highly compatible. For something as important as my future wife and family, I had to take some risk and expose myself to rejection, but I did so with some assurance that all was likely to go well.

And ditto for my clients. Not a single one of them, including even retired clients, is without higher-risk equities in their portfolios. But every one of them, including even the youngest among them, also has some form of cushion. It's wrong to think that only new retirees require downside protection. A young person who loses his job during a recession and needs to pay his mortgage, who then cracks open his retirement account, has just lost everything he's worked for. He pays taxes and penalties and with the rest pays his mortgage. So he too needs a cash reserve.

So to answer your question, Reggie, I'd put it this way. The reason it seems that I and my clients are thriving is that we're on a wealth accumulation train that includes no stops at two stations in particularly bad areas: One is called Insolvency and the other is called Instability.

In contrast, you and your clients are on a high-speed bullet train that goes faster and further, but jolts wildly, occasionally careening towards Insolvency and Instability, which is why you're not feeling great about your business right now and why some of your clients have unceremoniously left. What this means, in essence, is that even when times were great and everyone was making money, you were already headed for a crash. Throw a ball up in the air forcefully, it will surely rise high, but we all know it's coming down. Without a mechanism for cushioning its landing, it's going to fall hard.

STEPHENSON enters.

STEPHENSON

Hey Reggie.

REGGIE

Hi Robert. You remember Benjamin? He was in my trainee class. He worked with Joseph Pelowitz.

STEPHENSON

Yeah. I definitely recognize you. And I know I've seen Pelowitz's name, but I don't really know him personally. What's up, guys?

REGGIE

Benjamin was just offering me an interesting theory about our different wealth-management styles. If I understood it correctly, he suggests that the downside-protection that cushions all of his clients doesn't rise as fast as our more aggressive approach, but results in happier clients, whereas our approach, which leads to bigger numbers, also entails periods of extreme volatility and greater unhappiness. Is that a fair restatement, Benjamin?

BENJAMIN

In crude terms, yeah, that's the gist of it.

STEPHENSON

Crude is right. You're still young, Benjamin, so you've got time to figure this out, but in all candor, I pity anyone who thinks that way. Do the math. Let's say you know, you really know, how to properly cushion a portfolio, which is not always so easy to do in actuality. So in a brutal market crash like the current one, maybe your portfolios have fallen, say 25 percent, whereas ours have fallen 50 percent. I've been in this business long enough to tell you that that's just a blip on the radar long-term. And the proof is in our businesses. I managed $6 billion in assets until a short time ago. We've sunk to $3 billion, and that's no fun, for sure. But in due course, we'll be back at $6 billion and eventually $7 billion, $8 billion and beyond. Like I mentioned, I don't really know your former boss, Pelowitz, but I do know he's never once joined us for the Chairman's

Council annual top producers' retreat, much less our Bel Air Club for billion-level assets under management.

BENJAMIN

With all due respect, Mr. Stephenson, I don't think managing a billion dollars or more is one of Mr. Pelowitz's goals. It's certainly not my goal, which is to see all of my clients prosper, without a single one of them getting wiped out.

STEPHENSON

Our clients who stick with us will recover and be better off than ever. But I don't see how you can accept mediocrity on behalf of your clients. Our goal is excellence. Our job is to maximize client wealth. Like ants after a picnic, we don't leave even a crumb on the table.

BENJAMIN

But don't ants store way more food than they can ever eat? Meanwhile some other insects eat their food, and some other creatures eat *them*. Shouldn't we aspire to a balance between accumulation and enjoyment?

REGGIE

What I think you're not appreciating here is the value of excellence that our firm holds as an ideal. It's something we take very seriously. We're not exactly a jock shop, but we're determined to compete and win in every area: We aim for the highest possible returns, the highest possible assets under management and the highest possible service to our clients. Those are our firm's values.

BENJAMIN

I was never a top athlete like either of you two gentlemen. I'd never make it in your firm. But, for what it's worth, I'll never forget an incident that took place in my high school. One kid was the school's top swimmer but he constantly butted heads with the coach over a "me first" attitude and lack of consideration for the team. The coach brought a bucket of water to his side and told him to swish the water around. After the kid removed his hand, the coach took out a stop watch and said, "Let's see how long it takes for the waves created by the swishing to die down." At the coach's behest, the kid read the time. "26 seconds," he said. To which the coach replied, "That's how long it will take us to get back to normal after I kick you off the team."

That's kind of how I see this whole "highest returns" business. The stock market giveth, the stock market taketh. If we stick with stocks, we return to the average. Paradoxically, a cash cushion, which lowers the rate of the return by virtue of not being in stocks, can more than make up for that absence by buying in conditions of extreme bearishness, which is exactly what my clients are doing during this crash.

REGGIE

They're really doing that? We're finding many of our clients reluctant to get into this market, and not a few eager to get out.

BENJAMIN

Not one of our clients has expressed any interest in exiting their positions. And most of them are buying now. The ones who aren't are the ones who have not as yet set aside sufficient reserve funds, and they're kicking themselves.

In any case, it was nice speaking with you both. I've got to run now. Wishing you much success.

Leaves.

REGGIE

Interesting. Food for thought, in any case.

STEPHENSON

Thought-food isn't as filling as real food. As my old friend Mark Macher always says, "you don't sell, you don't eat." Well, at least not in Bel Air or Malibu.

STEPHENSON and REGGIE laugh.

SCENE 3

REGGIE pays a visit to BENJAMIN and SOPHIE in their home.

BENJAMIN

Doorbell rings.

Come on in, Reggie. Thanks for dropping by.

SOPHIE

Hi Reggie. Let me get you a cold drink. It's hot out there. Maybe you can stay for lunch too?

REGGIE

As much as I'd like to, I need to make this visit short. I've got a number of clients I need to call. Just wanted to drop by and bring this gift for the little princess. How are you and she feeling?

SOPHIE

We're all doing great. It helps enormously that Benjamin is taking a few weeks off of work so I don't have to manage the twins and a new baby all by myself.

REGGIE

Now I'm really jealous. Sam and I had to cancel our honeymoon last week because of the financial crisis. Robert says this is just one of those all-hands-on-deck times.

BENJAMIN

Oh. I'm so sorry to hear that.

REGGIE

Sam wasn't thrilled, but I was able to mollify her with the Chairman's Council trip to Tahiti in August. But I am bummed. It's kind of an anticlimactic way to begin married life. But what alternative do I have? Clients are still prone to jump ship. We just need to hang on till this crisis passes, and I'll get back to more normal working hours and better interactions with prospective clients.

BENJAMIN

You know, Reggie, here we are three years after we started advisor training today, and when I look at our fellow graduates, the ones who made it, my observation is that most earn way more than they would if they chose another profession and yet most are not all that happy.

REGGIE

I plead guilty, especially as I have to leave in a few minutes, which enhances my unhappiness at the moment. But before I do, I've got to ask you: To what do you attribute this phenomenon? I mean: money doesn't buy you happiness, but poverty doesn't either. And since it's beyond obvious that you two are not just successful, but also happy financial advisors, what's your take on this disconnect?

BENJAMIN

Well, one of the reasons Sophie and I are so happy – I mean professionally, that is to say, as financial advisors specifically – is we're among the very few we know – Mr. Pelowitz is another rare example – who take full advantage of one of the unique advantages this profession offers. We enjoy mastery of our time. We're not chained to our desks. Sophie is taking as much time off to be with the kids as she wants, and I'm taking off, initially, three weeks, but accepting calls that are important to the client. So far no one has booked any.

One of the attractions of this business is our independence, our ability to control our schedule. But look around, and most of our colleagues are not availing themselves of that option.

REGGIE

I wish I could. That doesn't work under our structure. You eat what you kill. Right now, the hunting opportunities are minimal, so it's a matter of fighting to keep our food supply through the next winter.

BENJAMIN

Do you realize you've become an ant?

REGGIE

The idea is starting to dawn on me.

BENJAMIN

I think for a lot of advisors, there's a confusion between corporate objectives and personal ones – both for you *and* for your clients. Stephenson is interested in how productive the clients are for *him*. But if your focus is on the client's happiness, satisfaction and fulfillment – the only return on investment that really matters – then you get to increase your own happiness, satisfaction and fulfillment ROI. The two go hand in hand.

REGGIE

I hear the argument, but I'm finding it difficult to absorb. Being top producers is fundamentally who we are. It's part of our identity. And it has worked for us. It's not just at Tilden Prescott that we're superstars. It sure feels that way in our client interactions, above all at Stephenson's annual Bel Air bash.

SOPHIE

If I may interject, Reggie, I find this discussion incredibly ironic. On our orientation, just before our formal training began and just before I left for Florida, Macher said very few of us – nine out of our class of 30 – would still be employed by the firm in three years' time. His prediction has proved prescient, as far as the numbers are concerned. But even though he seems to know his business, his reasoning seems a little off. He said the advisor-training survivors would be the ones who still have someone left to talk with. And that's the irony. You missed your honeymoon, and now need to head back to the office on a Sunday in order to make calls to clients you fear will bolt.

You're trying to appease them, even though you know they don't particularly want to speak with you right now.

Clearly nobody expected we'd be in a deep financial crisis three years ago when Macher made that statement, but the irony is that Benjamin and I, who are probably numbers 8 and 9 on the Tilden Prescott survivors' list, have a growing list of people to speak with: our clients, with whom we have warm relationships, and I would say a surge of new clients who are eager to speak with us precisely now, because they feel the more conventional money-management approaches have failed. Far be it from me, No. 9 out of 9 in our class to be telling No. 1 how this business works. I'm still figuring it out myself. Macher treated business development as a science, as something that can be broken down into parts, such that those who follow the instructions precisely, will succeed. But maybe that was an illusion after all. Your Hollywood clientele know a thing or two about make-believe. Along comes a financial crisis of historic proportions and that model begins to break down. And what remains is the *opposite* of show biz. It turns out that it's the substance of the contribution we make and the strength of the connection between advisor and client that fundamentally matter.

Thank God this crisis came just three years into our careers. Imagine what it would be like for you if this were 20 years into your career, how jarring it would be to make an adjustment if you wanted to, or needed to. What a shame it would be if this financial crisis passed without our discovering something about ourselves that could improve our own lives and careers.

REGGIE

That's it. I'm out of here.

BENJAMIN

Sorry we kept you so long. Sounds like you've got to get back to work.

REGGIE

I'm not going to work. I'm picking up Sam for a surprise honeymoon. I'll send Robert a postcard. I don't expect to come back the same person, and that should be a plus for my clients. Thank you Sophie for those words, and Benjamin for yours. If you think of it, please also send my warm regards to Pelo – please also thank Mr. Pelowitz for me. He is a wonderful advisor. How fortunate you are to have him as a mentor.

AFTERWORD

Financial advisors, like other professionals, are constantly being evaluated by their employers for their performance, and they in turn use the tools and data their companies equip them with to extract value out of their client "relationships." Establish a portfolio for a client, you may be seen as remiss if you don't follow up with an offer of a mortgage or personal loan. But the client may not have been seeking a mortgage, and your bringing it up inauthentically might not be perceived as a harmless effort to serve your client. You may give great retirement advice, but if you're randomly shilling loans, a doubt arises in the client's mind as to whether the retirement advice was just a sale, or precursor to an upsell.

A focus on "production" can be hazardous to client relationships because it can impart a transactional character to the service provided. If things later go wrong – say, the market goes down – the client can easily get angry or disappointed, a feeling that might not be aroused if the service provided was part of a financial plan in the context of a genuine relationship, and not a mere transaction. Selling and serving may involve the identical activities, but they *feel* different to advisor and client alike.

A primary emphasis on sales can be more lucrative. Set your mind to making money and you often will make money, which is a good thing of course. But this sort of focus can make relationships feel transactional, even if only in retrospect, as when markets fall and investors feel less good about the investments they now feel were "sold" to them. Many in the industry, aware of this problem, try to mask this feeling by cultivating a niche. Sharing a common passion for wine, gardening or golf does make relationships "stickier," as marketers are apt to say.

Nevertheless, when the commonality binding advisor and client weakens, the glue between them loses its adhesiveness. If golf ceases to be a passion for Joe Client, his connection with his advisor will be correspondingly weaker. What's more, the connection between wine and financial advice is actually artificial. So if portfolio performance is weak, the client's enthusiasm for the advisor's next wine-tasting event may wane.

An alternative approach to excellence involves the acquisition of wisdom, judgment and integrity by which the client understands the advisor's contribution to his success as prudent asset allocation and wealth-building rather than gnostic stockpicking, exotic products or razzmatazz marketing jargon.

This model contains two components: the first is expertise in financial planning rather than in wine or golf; the second is personal character. This is something you can't fake; it's something you build over time.

The sales model depends heavily on technology. Organizations generally want sales, so they develop apps to handle non-sales substantive areas of the business. It is astonishing what these programs can do. Their users not infrequently believe that they're a lot smarter than ordinary practitioners lacking these tools. But a computer is without a conscience; you can't enter the client's anxieties and other human concerns into the program. There's no one to talk to. This brave new world of artificial intelligence suffers from being...artificial.

What the financial advisory world needs more of is authenticity. Sales and sales tools are a legitimate part of an advisor's path toward excellence. The gallop of technology will not be bridled, but its pace and force will trample some investors some of the time. Arresting technological progress helps no one, but adding a human dimension can help everyone.

A unique challenge financial advisors face is that they work in an area of inherent volatility. The market goes up and goes down. This instability means that the market will not always stand by you. When that happens, you need to have your character stand for you. What you have worked on and achieved remains your constant advocate, silently reassuring clients they are in good hands.

When you authentically inject something of yourself into your interactions with the client, you further enhance that client experience. What's more, this effect can increase over time, since the ability to refine and develop one's unique self is limitless. People respond positively to authenticity. This is not about signaling, subliminal messages, the lure of cologne or perfume, all of which are inauthentic. It's about developing your natural gifts.

The specific path to excellence is your choice. You can achieve sales stardom, or you can become a paragon of your profession through your knowledge and character. Either approach will earn you accolades, and there may be overlap between them. But be mindful of the tradeoffs, and consider that the more authentic the advisor, the more contented the client.

ABOUT THE AUTHOR

Gil Weinreich has worked in the financial-advisor arena since 1997, as editor-in-chief of Research Magazine (and contributor to its ThinkAdvisor website) for 18 years and as Seeking Alpha's senior editor for financial advisor content and producer of its "SA for FAs" podcast for four years. The New York State Society of CPAs twice awarded its prestigious Excellence in Financial Journalism award to him for a monthly column he wrote on business ethics. Previously, he reported on international news for Voice of America (where he was awarded a newsroom writing award) and prior to that he worked as an editorial assistant at U.S. News and World Report. He currently serves as a consultant and content strategist for the financial services industry. He can be reached by:

E-mail: GilWeinreich@gmail.com

Website: GilWeinreich.com

LinkedIn: https://www.linkedin.com/in/gil-weinreich-302641/

Twitter: https://twitter.com/GilWeinreich

www.ingramcontent.com/pod-product-compliance
Lightning Source LLC
Chambersburg PA
CBHW050253220526
45465CB00002B/663